SHARED THOUGHTS

SHARED THOUGHTS

EDITED BY
MARK MAGEE

BOOK MARK PUBLICATIONS
61 Chingford Road Walthamstow London E17 4PW

Date of Publication
June 1997

Published in the UK by
Book Mark Publications
61 Chingford Road
Walthamstow
London E17 4PW

Telephone 0181 923 6183

© In this anthology Shared Thoughts, the Copyright of each Poem remains with the Poet

Printed by:
ProPrint
Riverside Cottage
Great North Road
Stibbington
Peterborough PE8 6LR

ISBN: 0 9528040 9 3

All rights reserved. No part of this publication may be reproduced or transmitted in any form or by any means, electronic or mechanical, including photocopying, recording or any information storage and retrieval system, or for the source of ideas without the written permission of the publisher.

CONTENTS

Page No

John	Ainsley	Jewel In The Sea	1
John	Ainsley	There Are Poets	2
John	Ainsley	A Blustery February Day	3
Ron	Amato	My Friday Night Love	4
Ron	Amato	Whistful Thinking (My Friday Night Love)	5
Ralph	Andrews	Shared Secrets	6
Maureen	Arnold	Country Tapestry	7
Susan	Aspinall	Change And Travel	8
Marvyn	Attwell	Little Old Lady	9
Dawn	Avery	Shared Thoughts	10
Janine	Ayres	Insomnia	11
Janine	Ayres	The Fox	12
Dolly	Baldwin	The Truth	13
Doreen	Banas	The Nightmare Unfolds	14
Tracey	Barrett	Our Problem	15
Jackie	Barry	Rome Before Romance	16
Chris	Bentley	Love	17
Andrew	Challen	Peer Group Pressure	18
Diane	Challis	Good Intentions	19
C.P.	Clarke	The Skull	20
C.P.	Clarke	Mirror Image	21
Valerie	Colbert	Who Was The Hero	22
Roy	Coppin	Winter Season	23
Margrit	Dahm	Image And Phantasy	24
Gemma	Davis	You For Me	25
Kathy	Davis	That's Life	26
Kathy	Davis	That Special Gift	27
Marion	Denmark	Goal	28
Claire	Dobson	Discovery	29
Lesley	Eldred	Clouds	30
Josephine	Enright	Waiting	31
Len	Evans	Eden To Eternity	32
Barbara	Eyre	Winter Spring	33
Zetoon	Fazil	Deep Inside	34

			Page No
Zetoon	Fazil	Keeping Me Down	35
Euma Santos	Fernandes	The Apple Of Your Eyes	36
Euma Santos	Fernandes	Snowballs	37
Jonathan	Field	Solace	38
Jonathan	Field	You Alone	39
Jonathan	Field	My England	40
Sheila	Finch	Roses For The Lord	41
Bruce	Fisher	Christine	42/43
Lynda	Fordham	Animal Thoughts	44
Lynda	Fordham	Innocents Betrayed	45
Christine	Fox	Mary Magdalene	46
Kelly Jane	Francis	A Key To Change	47
Val	Freya	To Love	48
Valerie	Gamble	My Feelings On Love	49
Dave	Gatrell	Can We Create Anything	50
Emma	Hainesborough	Captured	51/52
Aruna	Hamid	The Valley	53
George	Harrison	Piano Ocean	54
Ronald	Hiscoke	Valued Friends	55
Susan	Irwin	The Kitchen	56
Dennis	Johnson	The Song Of Life	57
Dennis	Johnson	Reflection	58
Richard	Jones	Questionnaire	59
Ron	March	Spring	60
Ron	March	Change	61
Edward	McFadden	Yugo	62
Edward	McFadden	The Chestnut	63
Edward	McFadden	If I Could Hunt The Hunter	64
Marilyn	Michaels	The Homecoming	65
Carmel	Nye	Adolescence	66
Constance	Osbourn	The River Of Life	67
Torsten	Payne	A Song For Love Unknown	68
Margaret Francis	Porter	Winter Days In Essex	69
Amanda	Potter	Cardboard City	70/71

Page No

Amanda	Potter	The Beauty of Life In Death	72
Ann	Pritchard	The Wedding	73
Nigel	Purssell	Dreams	74/75
Nigel	Purssell	Farewell To Love	76
Carol	Ratcliffe	Friendship	77
Nicki	Rhodes-Foster	'Divine Creator'	78
Anne E	Roberts	The Arrival	79
Ted	Rogers	Back To Basics	80
Ted	Rogers	Tales Of An Airman	81
Sharon	Rosenwould	Tears Of A Clown	82
Sharon	Rosenwould	Stand Back	83
	Sabby	My Memory	84
Maureen	Salmon	Another Riot	85
Brenda	Saxty	Discovery	86
Marco	Scarola	Whodinni's Dream	87
Jennifer	Sharp	The Silent Land	88
Gladys	Sharp	Home-Sweet-Home	89
Alison	Shaw	Monologue For A New Lover	90
Kim	Singh	Enchantment	91
William	Singleton	Flowers	92
William	Singleton	Clouds	93
Christopher	Stavrou	Winter Coming	94
Nicola	Stewart	Will You	95
Brian	Stoneman	Alive Again	96
Roger	Taber	Surfing	97
Mary	Tevlin	Midge	98
William	Tremlett	Things We'll Share	99
William	Tremlett	That Certain Age	100
William	Tremlett	The Wind	101
Marilyn	Ward	Seed Of Inspiration	102
Marilyn	Ward	Loneliness	103

			Page No
Julia	Wells	Message	104
Holli	Wells	A Hermit	105
Julia	Wells	A Tear	106
Marie	Williams	The Wind	107
Anthony	Williams	Indecent Behaviour	108

JEWEL IN THE SEA

Upon the cliffs of Atherfield
The sea spume spraying white
Down on the rugged beach, hand, eyes shield
Silvery sunrays reflect, so bright.

Sunset lowering in the sky
Beaming golden, streaky red,
Before the darkness, air is fresh so clean.

Beautiful the scene

And westward fading sunrays
Play on white cliffs of freshwater
Shadows of evening, hushed so peaceful
Its shades before us alter.

To the East, balckgang chine
Darkness of night rolls on
Hurriedly hills and cliffs do climb
Before the light of day is gone.

Jewel in the sea, This! Isle of Wight
Yarmouth, East Cowes and Ryde
Happy families, Sandown beach just right

Children scream in fun on roundabouts (or hide)

Ventnor and Shanklin rising high
The hills and dales, a glorious green
Peaceful walks in sunshine, blue the sky
This jewel in the sea, a joy when seen.

John Ainsley

THERE ARE POETS!

There are Poets, oh! so many
Various, and sometimes a few, Hilarious
Yet all Poets, write and know,
Their writing's to be precarious.

There are Poets, from College and University
Who learn and learn, and study Poetry,
From the like of Keats, Hardy, Wordsworth,
And of course The Bard himself
But what do they know? Of life and adversity.

There are Poets, who are a bore
To read their rambling's is a chore,
Words so long, hit's one's mind like a gong,
Once read, they rarely get an encore.

There are Poets, who cannot rhyme
Whose writing's they think sublime,
It's only in their mind to know,
What they have written, for them to crow.

There are Poets, who are Natural,
They never learned it, from their school,
Who see the Beauty all around,
So their words, bring out sight and sound.

There are Poets, whose words are,
Like a Painter's brush,
A picture portrayed, as upon a canvas,
Artistic writing's. They do not rush.

There are Poets, write with meaning whole,
Written from the heart and soul,
Words that bring much beauty, to the mind
An Artist, of another kind.

Yes! There are Poets

John Ainsley

A BLUSTERY FEBRUARY DAY

A blustery February day it is,
So windy, wet and warmer.
I feel the wind and rain upon my brow,
I am alive to the elements, just now.

It is not easy when one cannot see
And relies on feeling and hearing - it has to be.
People, many do not understand, or have no time to talk,
Or share a friendly word, that says I care.

So when the wind is knocking at my door
Saying 'I know you're there,'
I know I'm not alone.

The sun now shines through the window
And lightens the darkness of my room.
The wind has gone and so has the rain for a while.

February is a changeable month,
Cold winds and snow and rain again.
On yet another day it will be so sunny and warm,
Forgetting all about the winter storm.
Then! Spring will return once more.

John Ainsley

MY FRIDAY NIGHT LOVE

My Friday night love, I have no shame
I'm up for the count, let's get on with the game.
She beckons me, tempts me, I cannot resist.
In search of desire, I probe and insist.

My Friday night love, her tricks are consuming
She draws me, implores me, her passion assuming.
Away with convention, a signal that's tempting
I rise to the bait - like a fool I'm pre-empting.

My Friday night love, she taunts me and teases
She begs for a diamond, to discard as she pleases!
She leads me, concedes to me, I'm confused to her suit,
She's the Queen to my Knave - I'm a slave in pursuit!

My Friday night love, her demand is a double.
My thoughts are in turmoil, I fear I'm in trouble.
Perhaps an alert! The signal for take-out, I'm never quite sure?
I must bid to her favour - a heart to endure?

My Friday night love, invites me to slam!
My response to her Gerber - I'm all for pleasing my adorable ma'am!
My answer to deny, simply leads her on to explore!
Deuce Peter! What befalls me? I'm a madman! I can't take anymore!

My Friday night love has me locked in her room,
She's laid out before me, the deal is my doom!
She craves me to satisfy, I may not rise-up to par!
But this lady's not for denying - is this my bridge gone too far?

Ron Amato

WHISTFUL THINKING
(MY FRIDAY NIGHT LOVE)

I'm chastened by her Xmas wish
Within a cardbored gift, a query?
The doubt that duly crossed my mind
Has she at last begun to weary?
Of my reckless bids and feckless ways
'Two, holding hands,' no-way man!
I'll carry on as if to please
Besotted with her stayman!

The bridge I cross is all alone
I deviate for no one.
The hand I play is mine alone
Be glad that we have won some!
When I call at the Cedars Lodge
I do so as a saver,
Its not that I can do without
Be sure, I need her favour.

Last week she shared a winning theme
Her luck was with another,
But pray this intervention
Was not another lover.
I seek to share with her, a Blackwood aspiration
Restore our partnership again and accept this invitation.
Then longing her responsive call
To re-unite at the Grandslam Ball!

Ron Amato

SHARED SECRETS

When you were a child you shared secrets with a friend
Not any old friend but someone special to depend
With a sympathetic ear
To express thoughts without fear
Standing side by side no matter what befall
Not far away, in an emergency to call.

As a teenager life can be a little unsure
To share secrets, that person needs to be mature
Whoever that may be
Must be trusted you see
For at this delicate age a secret shared
Can only be absolute and never be impaired.

Marriage brings intimacy between husband and wife
A loving and caring relationship, a sharing of life
Nothing to be disclosed
Private thoughts closed
For these moments are precious in every way
To be kept within, but remembered day by day.

In later life when change seems to be the norm
When secrets shared with friends now gone, takes on a new form
Unfortunately it has to be
The secret shared is now free
And you are the sole person, the secret safe to keep
Until yourself succumb to that final sleep.

A shared secret has a limited span
Because it only touches those who are within the scan
This exclusive thought
Cannot be bought
For no price can be put on such an important issue
Because sharing truth, secrets and thoughts is friendship true.

Ralph Andrews

COUNTRY TAPESTRY

Driving through the Cotswolds,
You hope it will never end.
As wonderful views of the countryside,
Come into view different around each bend.
Foliage of striking colours, Russet Brown,
Gold, Yellow and Green.
Some of the most beautiful countryside,
That I have ever seen.
Villages and country lanes,
Edged with dry stone walls,
Streams that run through the valleys,
Gentle waterfalls.

Cottages with log fires,
And ceilings with oak beams,
Horse brasses, and copper plate,
Polished until it gleams.
Ancient churches, covered in vines,
With stained glass windows, that tell a story.
This is all part of the Cotswolds
With its charm and glory.
It really is beautiful, a country tapestry.
Oh yes, the magical Cotswolds will always
Hold a special enchantment for me.

Maureen Arnold

CHANGE AND TRAVEL

To unravel the problem of travel
To change the way of the car.
The petrol, the oil, and pollution.
Has endangered the world so far.

Electric's the way of the future,
And steam was the way of the past.
The way that the whole world is going.
Mean's that travels a thing of the past.

So you now change the colour
Of your vehicle.
From black, green, or red white
and blue.
With a clean wing and rusty old bonnet.
Four flat tyre's and dirty old boot.

Susan Aspinall

LITTLE OLD LADY

A little old lady, down our road,
Always sits in her chair,
She never seems to do much,
Except just sit and stare.

She watches all the children,
Going and coming from class,
And she is still sitting there,
When the last of them pass.

She hasn't got a husband,
Just a little cat,
And that always sits in the chair,
Where her husband sat.

I think how lonely she must be,
For no-one visits her,
She just has the cat to talk to,
As he gives a gentle purr.

I haven't see her recently,
I heard she may have died,
And though I never knew her,
I must admit I cried.

For though we argue quite a lot,
I still have my ma,
As most of us have family,
Which shows how lucky we are.

Marvyn Attwell

SHARED THOUGHTS

A chuckle and a giggle
You do the same to me
Yet all the bodies round us
See you so differently
You have such inner feelings
That only we can share
Arrogant and simply rude
Is as they see you there
If only they could get to know
The man that is inside
The day I grew to love you so
You took me as your bride
I've grown a little easier
Of remarks they all must say
And now we can communicate
And it's us that giggle of they.

Dawn Avery

INSOMNIA

Deep in the shadows of the restless night
Where slumber rules, to the sandman's delight
I am awake, pacing the floor
My eyes turned always, to the closed wooden door.

I begin to hear noises, outside my window pane
I lift my curtain, to stare at the road, again
But no one is there, the street stands alone
As the pain grips my heart, I inwardly groan.

The clock ticks on, seconds are like days
I pray for sleep, to escape in the haze
But is not to be as my thoughts rule my mind
As insomnia, does a broken heart remind.

The questions I ponder, at night in my room
As I pace the floor, lit up by the moon
Are 'Why did it happen?' and 'why did it end?'
As he was my love, as well as best friend.

Janine Ayres

THE FOX

The fox lay alone, upon the bracken floor
His body is broken, aching and sore
He sees the men now, as they come with their guns
But the fox has no energy to get up and run.

The hounds begin to sniff around the fox's den
Letting out excited squeaks, like little children
The fox tries to get lower, shaking with fright
Trying to hide, scared of the hounds delight.

A dog begins to growl, identifying the smell
All the dogs bark, like the hounds of hell
The fox is trapped alone, there can be no escape
He can do nothing now, except try to hide and wait.

The hound enters the lair, softly on his feet
Looking for something, to attack or eat
He spies the fox, and throws back his head
The fox realises that he will soon be dead.

The hunter enters the den, with his gun
With big yellow eyes, the fox looks upon the sun
It is the last time he will feel the pain
As down onto the floor, his blood does rain.

Janine Ayres

THE TRUTH

If for one day we spoke the truth, just imagine
What would happen.
For many times the things we say, are a habit
Forming pattern.
How are you? The question is asked, the reply is,
I'm alright.
When often this is not the case, we are really
In a plight.
Many times white lies are told, to spare somebody's
Feelings.
How would it be if the truth was told, instead of
Just concealing.
It might lead to drastic results, that could be
Rather shocking.
But is it right to hide the truth and inwardly
Do the mocking?

Dolly Baldwin

THE NIGHTMARE UNFOLDS

Trawling for fish; but the catch is poor
Waves are breaking on a polluted shore.
Lonely watcher looking out to sea -
Is it too late to change what has to be?
An empty space with an empty skyline
A world away from woods of beech and pine
The world as we knew it has ceased to be.
Lonely watcher looking out to sea.
Pollution - and waste has taken over
No one looks at wildflowers, grass or clover
No one worries about diesel fumes -
Around the town centre rising in plumes.
Every two seconds sees a plane in the air
With noisy pollutants creating a nightmare.
Lonely watcher looking out to sea
Turn back the pages of history
Do something now, before it's too late
If everyone tries we can alter our fate
Before earth's movement in a few years' time
Means the end of our world - yours and mine.

Doreen Banas

OUR PROBLEMS

Who do you share your thoughts with?
Is it someone who is positive?
Do they really listen to you?
Or just say something out of the blue.

Do they look at you and your face?
Or here there, any other place?
Nodding and shrugging at the wrong time
You may as well be there doing a mime.

But what about when the tables are turned
And they want to talk about what they have learned
They come around and knock on your door
Telling you they can't take any more.

You sit there politely offering tea
Saying 'its alright you can tell me'
You try not to look so interested, they weren't for you
But you can't you're not so rude.

You pat their back 'it's okay'
'You'll feel better another day'
They go home feeling what they have gained
And you are left feeling sad and drained.

Tracey Barrett

ROME BEFORE ROMANCE

Do not race to the Altar when young,
But travel the wide world instead,
Be on top of the Alps or the Andes,
And not the maternity bed.

Don't be frightened to differ from others,
If they won't go, then go it alone,
When your feet are not ready to settle,
Brave off to the Gulf Coast and roam.

Walk the length of The Great Wall of China,
Climb the height of Niagara Falls,
Then think of your friends and your family,
At the back of their small childrens calls.

Send postcards from Egypt and India,
Then, New Zealand, a 'Wish you were here,'
Which they will, whilst they're changing the baby,
Boyfriend in pub, with his beer.

Go to Paris, the city of lovers,
Ignore treacherous thoughts, 'I'm alone,'
You've not been to Goa or Cyprus,
Quick head for that boat, on to Rome.

But when thoughts start to turn toward Mother,
Las Vegas lights dull, not a shine,
Grab the first plane and fly home to England,
You've just reached your settling down time.

Jackie Barry

LOVE

Love is forever, love is like gold,
Love means sharing, with young and old,
Love is kindness, broken hearts and a rose,
Love isn't for those that just want to pose,
Love's like country music - a matter of taste,
Love isn't for those who do it with haste,
Love's like a mountain road - it never runs smooth,
Love's not for those in a photo booth,
Love is what your heart's set on,
Love's like a bad soap opera,
It goes on + on + on ....

Chris Bentley

PEER GROUP PRESSURE

We all make mistakes from time to time
Though we do not necessarily learn from them
As we are prevented from such a useful exercise
By not only our place in our own esteem
But also by that of our entire acquaintance
(Unless we can somehow construe our mistake as a joke)
(In which case we can both eat our cake and keep it)

But when we do make a mistake
And lack such a convenient escape from ourselves
We can well maximise our error by the pretence
That its what we really intended all the time!
If only to avoid the second-glance of the (probably) uncaring
Thus confining ourselves to the future of our second-best
Which could be far worse than what we ever once thought possible.

Andrew Challen

GOOD INTENTIONS

I saw this poster out one day
I thought 'What a good idea'
'Could you give a Guide Dog pup a home?
Its only for a year'

They said 'Its such a lot of fun
And we pay for everything too
Just give this adorable pup a home
That's all you have to do.'

I wish I hadn't seen it
I wish I'd walked away
Then my house was chewed and my arms were mauled
When the Guide Dog came to stay.

She wouldn't let me brush her
She wouldn't sleep at night
She wouldn't even walk down the road
Without putting up a fight!

They said 'You must be firm with her
You never must give in
You have to let her know who's boss
And never let her win'

She bit my husband, broke a tooth
What was I doing wrong?
'Please come and take her back' I cried
A year is far too long!

So if you see this poster
Just follow the golden rule
And don't look into those puppy eyes
'Cause it isn't fun at all!

Diane Challis

THE SKULL

'The Skull,'
That's what they called it,
The place where they took them.
A public and final humiliation.

A mound of earth,
A raised platform of suffering and pain;
The dying man's stage.
His final claim to fame.

They'd taunt as they marched
To see the dying men suffer.
A sick audience,
Only the close with a tear in mind.

How unkind was their crime,
And how vicious the sentence;
No torture so cruel
As the pain of Golgotha.

C.P. Clarke

MIRROR IMAGE

A mirror reflects what you see,
But what you don't see is me.
I'm staring out at you,
And copying everything that you do.

I'm your mirror image,
So what you see can't be,
Because what you are - is me!

So am I here?
Or are you there?

What is reality?

C.P. Clarke

WHO WAS THE HERO?

Was Jesus really the Hero?
Of that story which shows us the way,
If it were not for the bad man
Would He have had something to say,
We all play out part in the journey of life
Thru' the darkness of man made Hell
And the Heaven of which we are searchin
It's only but one thought away,

Judas forsook his share of the glory
And was condemned for ever to Hell,
But I believe he needed no glory
Neither did Jesus, the friend he betrayed
They just played their part in the journey of life
That will take us to Heaven from Hell,

Tis' in the pain and the glory
Tis' in the fear and the lies,
Tis' in the knowing that we are
A part of that we despise,
Tis' in the knowing that Judas is Jesus
And God and the Devil the same,
That will finely bring us together
No longer playing the game.
Although in man's eyes the action is the same,
So be thankful the Devil, he shows you the road
Forsaken' his place in Heaven's abode,

Tis' not in seekin' a far off land
Nether is it in Fame nor wealth,
The Heaven your seekin' lay closer to hand
In the Relationship you have with yourself,
And it's only but one thought away.

Valerie Colbert

WINTER SEASON

The season has now changed to winter the same time as every other
Year
Brings with it that abundance of magic landscapes so divine and clear.
Spring summer and autumn these other seasons had been and quickly
Past
Through experience we know this season for three months it will last.

Check the doors and windows cover garden plants that are dearly loved
And time to find the woollens the rubber boots overcoat hat and gloves.
Look over the water system making sure its been tightly lagged
Care for all your external animals check their food is safely bagged.

Woke up in the morning to attend our days work or school we must go
And find nature has surprised us all and covered this land with snow.
This splendid view before our drowsy eyes of her elegance and grace
We are glad to feast upon this scene that does make our heart to pace.

And so astonished where the time has gone it seems like only yesterday
Spring is sprung that ambience of white snow has now melted all away.
But let us not forget these months of magical splendour on this earth
For it will return as always each year its magnificent stately birth.

Roy Coppin

IMAGE AND PHANTASY

Image holds the key to truth
If by truth we mean reality
Phantasy is truth betrayed
But wiser sometimes than is said. -

A shadow lifts its hand and speaks:
'Do not betray reality,
But when you venture out to search
Do not stray, when two will merge!

Handle your precarious gift
With caution, subtlety and strife,
For when you come to truthful acts
You go beyond the simple facts.'

The shadow spoke and bowed its head
And vanished gracefully,
The image stayed in literacy
Revealing truth in phantasy.

Margrit Dahm

YOU...FOR ME

You see for me,
When I am blind.
You speak for me,
With words I can't find.
You hear for me,
When I fail to.
You express for me,
The right thing to do.

You smell for me,
The danger I'm in.
You touch for me,
My unforgiven sins.
You breathe for me,
So I won't die.
You do this for me,
To keep me alive.

You walk for me,
Where my legs can't go.
You carry me,
Through highs and lows.
You laugh for me,
When I want to cry.
You praise for me,
When I have tried.

You lift for me,
My spirits and hopes.
You comfort me,
When I can no longer cope.
You do all this for me,
Without you, I don't know where I'd be.

Gemma Davis

THAT'S LIFE

'That's Life' is a comment often heard when things are going wrong
Like a new hairdo that's ruined, cos' the wind and rain's too strong!

And the day you go out window shopping, with no money in your Purse
You see everything you wanted there, its enough to make you curse!

Late for work, you run for the bus just as the clock starts to chime
And you see the bus just pull away, cos' for once it came on time!

Only time passes for the next half hour, but with buses you discover
That when one finally comes along, so does another.... and another!

Your best jacket's in the cleaners, but when you get there the shop's
Shut
And when you hurry home to watch T.V. you find there's been a power
Cut!

At the end of the day when you're feeling tired and you've had enough
Trouble and strife
You walk thro' the door and there's your mother-in-law, oh well, I
Guess.....

'That's Life'

Kathy Davis

THAT SPECIAL GIFT

Can you think of something that's both serious and fun,
And is free entertainment when all is said and done?

You can use it in a song, a prayer and verses too.
To give hope to someone sad or for sharing dreams come true!

Yes, I'm sure you've guessed, after all there's not much choice.
Its that very 'Special Gift' we choose to call a 'Voice.'

Kathy Davis

GOAL

The ground was packed, the crowd was loud
As the teams came out to play,
The fans were really very proud
As they watched their team that day.

They'd followed them up and down the land,
Through weather hot and cold,
And once they'd listened to the band
The game could now unfold.

They yelled, they shouted and they sang,
The teams ran up and down,
'Please score a goal and if you can
Bring the cup back to 'The Town.'

Only two more minutes to go,
The ball is in the net,
Now, at last, our team must know,
That is their best goal yet.

Marion Denmark

DISCOVERY

With life as complex as it is,
We discover new things every day,
About the future and of a time which has past us by,
But we always have to question Why?

We study animal traits,
Dig for pieces of the past,
We discover too, about the sky,
With the rockets that soar way up high.

We still have so much more to learn,
New discoveries are waiting for us out there,
Discovery will go on, if we live or die,
So, do we have to always question why?

Claire Dobson

CLOUDS

Billowing, unusual shape formation,
Sunshine, white clouds pure, unfettered;
Emotive patterns, weather disturbance,
Pending storm, aggravated, unsettled.
Cloud covering a humid, sultry sky,
Fresh air endeavouring to filter through;
Breeze arrives and shifts the blanket,
Clouds interrupting a sky now blue.
Clouds culminating in an angry mood,
Summoned by lightning in vivid flash;
Floods threaten, following a downpour,
Everyone drenched in a united dash.
Sky now settled, clouds are kind,
Gently traversing across the sky;
Tumbling shapes in various guises,
Nature's creations all reaching high.

Lesley Eldred

WAITING

In the beginning...
There was silence
Filled with the pregnant expectancy of his glory.
We saw it once,
Glimpsed fleetingly in a woman.
Declared amongst us,
Shining sparks against the sun,
Warming us with his love.
Surely my heart ached for you.
And now I wait,
Indeed we all wait; in trembling fear or joy.
Indeed the womb of this wide world awaits a unison,
Aching in travail for he who is to come.

Josephine Enright

EDEN TO ETERNITY

A spiritual monopoly, where the senses and feelings are
Elevated beyond the five senses we now know,
Into a realm of wonderment, of ecstasy,
Where man is transformed into a being of integrity,
Of high moral standards, where he knows that to sink into
The lower realms, is to stay in the outer darkness.

To be high is just to be at peace with oneself and with every
Part of one's being, environment and atmosphere.
To enjoy the ultra - sensitive passions of mindful pleasure,
Felt only in the mind's unique corridors of timelessness,
Where all, where everything transcends thought.
To try to describe would be futile, but a sharing of the senses
Can be beneficial to the occupants, to as many as would feel the
Vibrant warmth that lives hidden within the mind's passages.

Look, no, not look but feel, go inside, deep within its crevices
For the secrets that lie within. An abundance of wealth and treasures
Are awaiting you. Far greater than all the world's material offerings.
A colourful kaleidoscope of shapes and sights, waiting to be harnessed,
Waiting to be called upon, to be used. What good is storage,
If not used it rots, it decays.

Oh, what a waste, precious are the jewels that lie within,
Pretty are its colours, sweet is the fragrance.
Open up the gentle buds and taste the substance, the sweet, sweet
Nectar.
Listen to the murmuring's of the soul. Listen, Listen.

Len Evans

WINTER SPRING

Snowflakes like precious jewels
Fall onto the ground.
To make a blanket pure and white
To cover all around.

The sky so grey, the landscape bleak.
Here winter shows its beauty deep.

The Robin as if just reborn
Sits looking at the cold grey dawn.
Whilst here and there up on a hill
Some vagrant sheep stand, silent and still.

Where once fervent green pastures rolled anew.
O'er hill and dale now all is hidden to view.

The wind unseen bites hard and cold
And many a traveller hardy and bold.
Has gazed in bewilderment, wonder and awe
At the beauty of winter, so naked and raw.

But all too soon O'er woodlands and field.
The rain kisses the snow and spring is revealed.

Barbara Eyre

DEEP INSIDE

I've kept it all in
For so long.

I've kept telling myself
Lies
Saying everything is all right
Looking brave
Looking strong
But, I was wrong.

Now, I'm letting it go
Crying isn't weak
Showing my feelings
Isn't deep.
Getting Grips
Holding on
Trying to be strong

But, I don't know for how long.

Zetoon Fazil

KEEPING ME DOWN

I feel like I'm drowning
I'm in it too deep -
For anyone to notice
No one can hear
My screams
No one can hear
My cries
My fears are keeping
Me inside
I struggle - I fight.
I want to stay alive.
Just when I think I can.
Something drags me
Back down.

Zetoon Fazil

THE APPLE OF YOUR EYES

I don't know whether I still am
The apple of your eyes.
I ran for many days, months and years,
From your presence.
I build castles and someone else's dreams,
And the wind undid them,
Blowing the ashes.
I was re-born dressed as a phoenix!
Immersed in a drop of water!

I saw your eyes from afar,
When they were mine!
Your eyes when they were mine,
Stripped the soul and confessed emotions!

I stopped in time and asked myself,
Will I still be the apple of your eyes?
If the golden dreams still live on.
Certainly they will never get old.
If the feeling screams from inside,
I give up then I just quit,
May the Present come to pass.
Without any delay, without waiting.

I want to see and live this meeting,
Let myself be,
Naked and eager,
Drunk in the insatiable
Thirst of love!
Love, which conquered winds and storms,
And not even the waters,
Were able to drown it!

Euma Santos Fernandes

SNOWBALLS

To find out as the snow falls
The joy of your children!
The freshness of the full smile
And the hungry gladness
Coming up as the sun!
I could taste the snow flakes
The flavour of the tremendous yeal
Which reveals the emotion of these people!
Stripping up the warmth of life!
Contagious...inviting us
To the snowballs toast!

And in this play
To keep the expression of ecstasy!
Ho! To see you London partying
Dressed as a bride,
Warmly dressed with all charms
At daybreak!
Awakening forgotten and yellow smiles
Amid dull bodies and faces
No shine, no colour!

Ah! Snow, came and awaken my beloved,
Loosening the treasures of all charms!
Opening up heaven's doors,
Cheering her up, fill her with joy!
Ho! London, let me contemplate you
I will keep this moment
The streamer and confetti of your carnival!
And for the rest
Accept the loving eyes and heart
Of this mortal one
Seeing you beautiful in body and soul
Delighted, making yourself loved!

Euma Santos Fernandes

SOLACE

My window calls me to it,
As from the roar I hide,
The beauty there before me,
Takes me to its side.

Gone are the cares around me,
What tranquillity I find,
From that tiny window,
The view is oh, so kind.

Peace descends upon me,
My tree does this for me,
Its arms outstretched to the skies,
Such beauty do I see.

The branches gently swaying,
Caressed by the soft warm breeze,
The one lone apple seated there,
Seated there to tease?

I feel an urge inside me,
I long to climb that tree,
To sit among its leafy arms,
Feel its love round me.

Loved ones seem so far away,
So to my room I hide,
What does that window do for me,
How can I describe?

Peace descends upon me,
As from the roar I hide,
The beauty there before me,
Draws me to its side.

Jonathan Field

YOU ALONE

I gave my heart so tenderly,
'twas all I had to give,
Why did you not take it,
How am I to live?

A rose you put into my hand,
I thought it brought your love,
But it flew away from me,
As flies the gentle dove.

How can I retrieve it,
What do you ask of me,
My love for you is in my face,
For all the world to see.

Jonathan Field

MY ENGLAND

So small she lies amid the seas,
But her strength I know,
For I have seen her fight for right,
Yes, fight the greatest foe.

Her heart be pure, so doth her soul,
For with my eyes I've seen,
Her doors have opened wide to all,
Who in need have been.

She gave them love and shelter,
Helped them again to rise,
Oh my England! though so small,
Much bigger be thy size.

Jonathan Field

ROSES FOR THE LORD

Let us be roses
Growing for you
In your garden so holy
'neath the Heavenly blue.

Fill us dear Father
With your love so sweet
That the fragrance overflows
On our Saviour's feet

Raindrops slide off our velvety face
As you tenderly lift us
With your Heavenly Grace

We yield ourselves forth
To your throne above
May you receive us Father
As a 'Bouquet of Love'

We offer ourselves for your fullest delight
So Father please bind us with your love so tight
Your arms like a ribbon that enfold us just right
That together we pray
The fragrance shall be
A beautiful essence forever to Thee!!!!

Sheila Finch

CHRISTINE

I think of you and sadly see the treasure that I could have had
I let you slip away from me and leave me for another lad
I was a frightened virgin boy and so afraid of your desire
I was unable to employ the nerve to raise our passion higher.

For months you waited patiently but love to me was something new
If I'd have spoken honestly perhaps you would have helped me through
I should have treated preciously someone as wonderful as you
And should have met you frequently, I really didn't have a clue.

A friend of mine came on the scene and he thought he would make a
Try
His romance could not have been if I'd have been a better guy
The word got round then back to me and I knew that my time was done
It left me hurt and so lonely, I lied pretending it was fun.

I should have held on more than that, and maybe you'd have been my
Wife
Instead I acted like a prat regretted it for all my life
I'd met the star in my life's show then watched you marry to my friend
I thought my love would fade and go but love for you would never end.

I thought about the hand I'd miss, the hand I used to hold so tight
I knew that I'd no longer kiss the lips I used to kiss goodnight
I knew I'd miss those lovely eyes, those brown eyes clashing with my
Blue
But most I'd miss the greatest prize, the life I could have had with you.

The greatest thrill my whole life through on Easter Sunday Sixty Six
You asked if I would dance with you a better date I'd never fix
I never dreamed I'd ever meet someone I'd think of like I do
And nothing yet has ever beat the memories that I have of you.

When we were only Seventeen I should have kept you by my side
I won't forget our love Christine to be your man filled me with pride
Through ever year you've touched my mind a person I would always
Miss
A better girl I'd never find, I kissed a dream then lost the kiss.

Bruce Fisher

ANIMAL THOUGHTS

I used to roam the jungles
Sleep in the branches of luscious trees
But my future now hangs in jeopardy
For man is desecrating these

My home was full of varied minerals
In its depths I freely swam
This has now been polluted by oil slicks
Caused by the carelessness of man

I once built my nest, high in the mountains
Hunting a wide terrain
Now progress has altered all of this
With the introduction of acid rain

We lived upon this earth before you
Without technology we survived
By threatening our environment
It's your children you'll deprive.

Lynda Fordham

INNOCENTS BETRAYED

I can still recall that fateful day
When one single shot, took your life away.

Innocent child so full of fun
You did not deserve to be killed by a gun.

There is your school presumed safe and protected
That maniacal crime could not be detected.

Silent, intense following instructions
No one could know this would lead to destruction.

Heaven transformed suddenly into a hell
This is John's blood see where he fell.

Here stood my son, there sat my daughter
Gone, not forgotten, taken by unwarranted slaughter.

They were the innocents, unblemished and sweet
Wiped out by the crime that lives in our streets.

How many petitions, what percentage of fuss
Must we arouse, before those in charge listen to us.

Ban all the weapons, thugs legally buy
To use on the helpless, and leave them to die.

Take away all the drugs, the impressionable use
Help them to live, instead of abuse.

Alert us to danger, make us detect
Let us stand by our principals, resume self respect.

We want to live in a world safe and kind
Free of sick people, hell bent on crime.

Lynda Fordham

MARY MAGDALENE

She traded love and coined men's passion,
Dealt with lust in the old profession.
She beguiled men with her smiles,
Took their money with her wiles.
She toppled Kings, she plied her trade,
For lesser men she dug a grave.
And yet no guilt was found within,
The soul of Mary Magdalene.

She was reviled by the good wife,
And yet they lead a similar life.
But she is honest with her game,
The other marries for her gain,
She has one man to bear her load,
The only soul that she can hold,
She is the judge who's stone is aimed
To outcast Mary Magdalene.

But why is she the one to blame?
Don't we all bear a similar shame?
For this may come as a surprise,
We are all whores when paid the price.
So think before you cast a stone,
The sin is not just hers alone,
For none of us is without sin,
Forgive us Mary Magdalene.

Christine Fox

A KEY TO CHANGE

I used to think a few years back,
The beliefs I had were fine.
My materialistic attitude,
A leviathan of our time.
There were a set of principles,
The main- financial wealth.
I didn't conduct my life the right way,
No real concern over health.
And then a series of months passed,
Before realisation struck me.
The door I'd always thought would be closed
Was open and I had the key.
There's still many people out there today
Who think triumphs make them a star.
But they're no better humans than you or than me,
No chance....no way by far.

Kelly J. Francis

TO LOVE

Our lips touch, soft and warm
Stirs the juices, deeply born,
Hands caress each other wildly,
Reaching points, erratically, blindly.

Deep emotions, stirring and rising
Bodies twisting, turning, burning
Moans of pleasure, we express
The ultimate climax we compress.

Physically expressing our love
On another level, way above
Satisfying our loving feelings
Receiving and giving sexual healing.

Val Freya

MY FEELINGS ON LOVE

How can I express my feelings on love?
Does she come with the air as she floats from above?
As love travels along, does she move with the wind?
Does she really take flight like a bird on the wing?

Love ripples through music like waves in a stream,
And gives us incentive to laugh and to dream,
So how can we stop love from drifting away?
By treating her gently with care every day.

How elusive love is, yet how quickly she grows,
Like the kiss of the sun shapes the face of a rose.
If love is our nature, then love we can find
In eyes all around us, in all of mankind.

Valerie Gamble

CAN WE CREATE ANYTHING

Can we create with positive thought
Anything's possible if often sought
But personal gain is usually from greed
Ask yourself first, do you really need.
From personal wealth and enough to survive
Which one of these people is truly alive!

If it's a want and not really needed
Then this message you have obviously not heeded
So yes we can create anything with the power of good,
And if the message is understood!

Dave Gatrell

CAPTURED

Captured and tortured, bound and gagged,
Using iron bars, or a dirty rag.
Ropes round our ankles, ropes round our wrists,
While were defenceless, they punch with their fists.
Kicks in the stomach, blows to the chest,
They think its a game, where they laugh and jest.
When we are weak, and spread on the floor,
They come at us laughing, to give us some more.
Our energy is gone, we lay unaware,
All they can do, is stand there and stare.
Stare at our suffering and obvious plight,
We have no power to rise and fight.
When the pain and the torture begin to ease,
The enemy come back to taunt and tease.
They laugh at our heartache, they think its a game,
They think its their duty, they're not to blame.
We huddle together as our bodies grow cold,
Like lonely, stray sheep, gathered in a fold.
We're thrown on the cattle trucks, with the aid of a ramp,
The pains just beginning as we head for the camp.

We are treated like dirt, like the scum of the earth,
Like disused objects of little or no worth.
We arrive at the camp, the wrought iron gates,
Before they slammed shut, I determined my fate.
Now my fate is determined by the enemy,
The enemy I now know will destroy me.
We are thrown in a heap, in the gravel and grime,
The bodies around me, whimper and whine.
As we gather together and observe our new hell,
We are suddenly struck by the stench and the smell.
The smell of disease, the dying, the dead,
I can smell the trauma, I can see only red.
The anger I feel, building strength inside,
A new hatred I've found which I know I must hide.
All I can see are flashlights and barbed wire,
And soldiers who laugh by the warmth of the fire.

Surrounded by guns, we shiver and shake,
The corpses around us, as thin as a rake.
Their faces like death, with no emotion,
No love, no caring, no loyal devotion.
Unhuman, detached, scars from the pain,
If they survive this torment, they'll never be the same.
Their bodies will be discarded when they die;
But their souls will remain to uncover the lie,
Uncover the truth; let the horrors be known,
But their souls cannot rest, we can hear them roam.
We know what they search, they long to be free,
But surely not as much as me.
I don't know if I'll live or die,
But for the first time in my life, I want to cry
The tears, the fears, the pain I feel,
The hellish nightmare begins to seem real.
I look behind at the alive and dead,
My once active body, has turned to lead.
The bodies I see, whether breathing or not,
Are dumped in mass graves, just to be forgot.
They once had honour, dignity, pride,
But terrified, they cower, they hide.
How can a human race be so cruel,
Whoever gave them the power to rule?

Emma Hainesborough

THE VALLEY

As I walked through the valley
Beside the glittering brook
Its flow my cares for the moment took
And as I crossed over the bridge of wood
After long, in peace, my world still stood
Not a sound was heard
Of cuckoo or any bird
Only a gentle breeze I felt
Like wax, the heart did melt
Sitting in this solitary place
God in nature I embraced
Eternity I could spend here
And stillness of life share
The brook adorned with moon's reflection
Mingled in love and full affection
In silent harmony it all seemed
As if I had all things gleaned.

Aruna Hamid

PIANO OCEAN

Live this moment
Savour this day
Tomorrow is indifferent
In our unfolding history

As the Ocean is deep
So too are these feelings
That break within me
You will always find
A special friend in me

Lingering sounds that stir
Unseen from the light of day
A rare unstoppable passion
Released from the swell
On the rocks of crashing waves

Just like a key
That strikes a chord
Deep within me
An erosion of time
Crystal clear
Yet so sublime.

George Harrison

VALUED FRIENDS

Those loyal and trusted individuals we recognise as friends
Who, steadfast like a rock and on whom we can depend.
With love and tender assistance reach out and all agreed
Acceptance of their sincerity which binds and never frees.

Those wondrous companions help with the complexities of life
Many are the instances when burdens cause such strife.
That friend was destined to assist and alleviate the wrong
Resourceful in their administration returning to a song.

So great a friendship and the confidence acquired
Each from whom no secrets are hid as they are admired.
Each thought a wonderful companion thus was greatly inspired
Acceptance of a will on all accounts never failure desired.

This friend is worth more than anyone might expect
They know the best and worst of us and never ever reject.
They never cause harm or pain as they soothe the tired brow
A blessed possession never to regret perfection never dour.

They give their whole attention when we are feeling low
They then make us feel more comfortable and how their treasures glow.
They have the art to manipulate and return us always to see
That they are indispensable a joy held in esteem.

Wholesome perfection is found in such individuals as these
Attending to our flimsy whims their aim always to please.
We could go on extolling their virtue as we are proud to portray
That friend who loves us dearly will never fade away.

Ronald Hiscoke

THE KITCHEN

When God created man
It was not in His plan,
To cook or clean or do the washing up,
But Adam and his wife
Opted for a life of strife
And a kitchen was designed to clutter up.

This kitchen now is here
To provide the cup to cheer
And to cook for hospitality.
Each person enters in
To give glory to the king
By serving others with humility.

So serve Him with good grace
And take care of this place
And share responsibility.
Clean up as you go
So that God will know
We honour Him for our prosperity.

Susan Irwin

THE SONG OF LIFE

Life has played its tune to me, and I did not sing along.
Sometimes the tempo was to slow, sometimes fast and strong.
At times the tune was happy, often it was sad.
And when it wandered way off key, it was very, very bad.
Now that it is getting to the end I recognise the tune.
The tune it was my very own, now, far too late I knew.
Life could have been so different, I could have sung along.
And recognised my souls desire to value right from wrong.
To regulate, and calm the pace. To value time, and value place.
To see again, with opened eyes, the most important things.
I should have heard the tunes around. And listened to their song.
Those faintly singing far away of suffering and wrong.
And to the wondering tunes of children, as they softly sing their songs.
I should have heard the tune, he played, so many years ago.
To that song the Master sang as he tried to let us know.
Perhaps it is not too late to listen to that tune again.
To try and sing the last refrain, before its finally gone...

Dennis Johnson

REFLECTION

I look in the mirror. What do I see?
I see an old man looking at me.
Where went the youth. Firm flesh unlined?
Where went the sparkle. Once in those eyes?
All that he dreamed of. Was never achieved.
A nightmare of war, was all he received.
A youth that was wasted. In warring lands spent.
The memory to linger. For years, to torment.
I look in the mirror. Now clearly I see.
The old man was youth. At the wrong time to be.

Dennis Johnson

QUESTIONNAIRE

When a loved one dies, does love linger on?
Can a ship sail the seas if the sea's all gone?
How can birds fly when they did not invent their wings?
Can a man be born poor? Be crucified? Be King of Kings?

Is black such a strange form of colour?
So different from white that they hate one another?
Is it good to be kind in a cruel way?
When a comedian you mock at to make him pay?

If a man takes his life is he a coward for dying?
When your son fails an exam do you say he's not trying?
If your wife has a child and you have fifteen others,
Do you wish she'd married not you but one of your brothers?

How can war for some be a profitable fling?
They fight with arms to lose legs and most other things.
Are here not many exceptions to every single rule?
Is it not then low democratically overruled a man a fool?

Can a man be kind while having roots in an animal past?
Is it good to be always first, sometimes better to be last?
Is co-operation taking over from competition in a wonderful way?
Do you know where you are going? Or are you going astray?

Do you live just to die? Is your heart always singing?
Can you sell your soul without even buying?
Is your life better by doing a good thing here and there?
Have you the mind? The heart? The soul? Of a questionnaire.

Richard Jones

SPRING

How delicate comes the spring to warm the cold
This left by winter's winds and snowy cover
Push forth the buds in search of light and sun
This surely is the time for every lover
New babies, flowers and dreams, to realise.
Let all of this come, hold it dear.
Let spring bring this to fill our eyes
Come spring bring buds of peace, not shutes of fear.

Ron March

CHANGE

Once standing proud with woven top
Reflecting gold on a summer's day,
Perhaps at dusk a couples hide
Warm afternoons, brought young to play.
First a castle, then a ship
Sliding down to land in hay,
Shouting farmer from a field
The cast now scampering, to get away.
The golden strands that made its form
Took the toll of play, and had to yield
But better then than today
Just a plastic roll, left in a field.

Ron March

YUGO

An empty sky
As the sniper sleeps
Silent roads
As the mother weeps
Shattered ruins
A poignant reminder
A trail of havoc
Left behind her
Warring factions
Blind to peace
Crucified a nation
They fought to keep.

Edward McFadden

THE CHESTNUT

One by one they fall
Fruits to the land
Cast by the winter's scorn
Forced to abdicate their lofty perch
On the ground they lay forlorn.
A brooding sky races on
Stealing the light of day.
The forest sings her eerie song
The marshland sways in time
On a bed of leaves red and brown
There lay the fruits
That once were the chestnuts crown.

Edward McFadden

IF I COULD HUNT THE HUNTER

The pack closes in
Ready for the kill
The scent is stronger
Blood will spill
Tired limbs scream for a rest
Maternal instincts put to the test
The hungry are waiting.

Just as the jailer holds the key
Now barbarians bring her to her knees
A once proud mother thinks of her young
Perhaps it will be quick, hope's its not long
The hungry are waiting.

Flesh is ripped, fur is torn
Redcoats gather no tears are borne
Its not that far from her safe haven
Just a little further to where
The hungry are waiting.

Edward McFadden

THE HOMECOMING

I'll need no angel
When my time has come,
To help me find my way
To my heavenly home.

I'll need no friendly face,
No once known friend
To comfort me,
At my seeming end.

I'll need no pressure
Of a tender hand
To reassure me.
No angelic band
Needs guide me
To that summer land.

I'll need no advocate
To plead my case,
For as I gaze at last
On His forgiving Face,
Who through my earth life
Blessed me, with His grace,
And with whom in dreams of Heaven
I seemed to roam,
My spirit will fly free and swift,
To its remembered home.

Marilyn Michaels

ADOLESCENCE

Twelve, thirteen, fourteen, fifteen,
Difficult days indeed.
Parents nagging on and on,
They just don't know my needs.

Make your bed, Tidy your room,.
That's what I hear each day.
They just don't care what's on my mind,
What can I possibly say?

The raised eyebrows when I get dressed,
They don't approve you see.
Not lady-like enough for them,
How boring can they be.

'Eat the right food,' 'cut out the junk,'
'Development's taking place.'
On and on and on they drone,
They won't get off my case.

When I get home from school each day,
I'm questioned on my grades.
'Do your homework,' 'Learn for your tests,'
My path is clearly laid.

Understanding's all I need,
But pigs are sure to fly
Before the time will ever come
When we see eye to eye!

Carmel Nye

THE RIVER OF LIFE - THE RIVER AND I

The river flows and takes along with it,
The dirt and debris of the darkest day.
It leaves behind the freshly washed river bed,
Sparkingly clean for a bright new day.
So start each morn with a fresh clear conscience,
Put behind you the previous day;
What has gone has passed beyond you,
Don't let it spoil yet another day.
Lift up your hearts and sing God's praises;
Rejoice at the dawn of day,
You can be sad, or you can be joyful,
You have the choice for each new day.

Constance Osbourn

A SONG FOR LOVE UNKNOWN

As I picture her, I often wonder,
Whether 'tis plain lust or manic ardour,
That imbues her with my viewed perfection,
For she alone needs no correction,

Her face I see still, when turned away,
As a burned image of the sun does stay,
And conjured visions of flower filled dells,
Accompany her name that tolls like a bell,

There's echoes of her in all great things,
A sunrise at dawn with the birds that sing,
Yet within her heart, no love does grow,
For this is a song for a love unknown.

Torsten Payne

WINTER DAYS IN ESSEX

How can they hate the winter,
When our Earth is so beautiful?
I sit at my window rejoicing,
In the sights, shapes and colours I see.

Such shades of colour in the garden,
From yellow to darkest of green.
The hedges light tipped 'gainst the background of grass,
Very soon the new growth will be seen.

They say 'What a dreadful morning!
What a lot of rain we've had!'
But the reservoirs still are very low,
And rain should make us glad.

'It's miserable weather,' they tell us,
'Dull and foggy, day after day!'
But oh, the beauty of a mist shrouded tree,
On a quiet, still, peaceful day!

They say, 'How I hate the winter,'
But they don't really mean it, I'm sure.
For endless, continuous sunshine,
Must very soon lose its allure.

So let us rejoice in the winter,
And enjoy the delights to be had.
While Nature is resting, we'll rest from the gardening,
Look forward to spring and be glad.

Margaret Francis Porter

CARDBOARD CITY

My house is the largest on the block
Made from a large Cornflakes box
For furniture, alas, I have none
My life on the streets has only just begun.

I used to have everything when I was in my prime
But things change with the passing of time
A house, car, job, and a beautiful wife
I'd wake up every morning and think 'what a wonderful life'

Then thanks to the government, mortgage payments rose
Electricity, gas, I was paying through the nose.
That's when the rows started, between me and my wife
There was poison creeping into my wonderful life.

One day, to his office the boss summoned me
'I have to put you off, there's no other way, you see
The recession has finally brought me to my knees.'
'Please keep me I'll do anything' I heard myself plea.

All the way home, I knew this was the end
Not for a failure would my wife want to tend
To save her embarrassment I packed my case and went
And for the first few days I slept inside a tent.

One day when I was out, looking for a job
Some other down and outs came along to rob
They took my tent and all my things
I stood there aghast as alarm bells did ring.

Please, don't ignore the people who are out there living rough
Believe me, their life may have suddenly got tough
They don't necessarily choose to be where they are
Maybe they once drove around in a fancy car.

So now I find myself, living in cardboard city.
People who were once like me, look down at me with pity.
How do I now get a job, without a fixed abode
When my address is just a box at the side of the road.

Amanda Potter

THE BEAUTY OF LIFE IN DEATH

Slowly twisting and turning a leaf flutters to the ground
And colours everywhere are changing all around,
Faded greens and yellows, also brown hues too
Looking like a picture postcard, all covered in morning dew.

In my bed I lay, looking out at the view
Knowing my time here, is now almost through.
Its funny how you never notice the beauty all around
Until you know for sure in life exactly where you're bound.

It doesn't seem so long ago when the doctor said to me
'I'm sorry but its terminal I can do no more you see.'
Everything seems so important, the birds migrating overhead,
Its a shame we don't cherish these things until we're nearly dead.

I'll never see the snow again, laying white upon the ground
Sparkling on trees and bushes, like diamonds all around.
Or watch the world come alive the moment Spring is here,
To see nature's things turning green, I just can't stop the tears.

Watching a rose budding, until it opens into full bloom
The scents coming through the window filling up the room.
My eyes slowly close as sleep at last comes
And my final thoughts are, my time here is now done.

Amanda Potter

THE WEDDING

The church bells are ringing,
There's a wedding you know,
So around the village I must go.
To see the bride and the bridegroom too.
And to see if I know who is who,
There's quite a crowd to this one,
Looks like the whole of the village has come.
I do believe it's our village Queen,
Quite the prettiest I have seen.
Long flowing dress and two bridesmaids in blue,
Looking so nervous... not sure what to do.
Her Dad looks so proud as she holds on his arm,
He kisses her cheek to make her feel calm.
The organ is playing as she walks down the aisle,
She is not quite so nervous... she managed a smile.
Her fiancé is standing with the best man,
As she gets nearer he holds out his hand.
They take a few steps and kneel at the altar,
Her mother is crying with joy for her daughter.
Dad looks like he has a tear in his eye,
As he fiddles around with his bow tie.
The church bells are ringing,
The doors open soon,
Then husband and wife go on their honeymoon.

Ann Pritchard

DREAMS

I can't stop being in love with you,
Though God knows how hard I've tried,
But these feelings that I have for you
Just cannot be denied.
It's not as though you led me on,
Or trapped me with deception,
You admitted you like handsome men,
Can't I be an exception?
I've seen you drunk, I've seen you drugged,
Or both, and off your face,
Yet to me you're the most perfect
Member of the human race.
I've watched you in the morning,
Still half asleep and drowsed,
Yet the vision of such loveliness
Always gets me aroused.
There's nought for you I would not do,
I'd die to have you by my side,
Forever to share life with you
Would fill my heart with pride.
I've seen you laugh, I've seen you cry,
And I've seen you mad as hell -
I've spent all of my pennies
In your wishing well
How do I get you to return
The love I feel for you,
Even pretend, for just one night,
That you love me too.

My eyes are damp with sorrow
As alone, of you, I dream,
How wonderful a couple
We'd make on life's long stream.
So come to me, my darling,
And beside my body lay,
Or I'll remain a crazy fool
Who for these dreams must pay.

Nigel Purssell

FAREWELL TO LOVE

'Twas once said that London town
Made the world go round and round,
While for some this statement's true,
The centre of my world is you.

Unworthy though this soul may be,
My heart I gladly offer thee,
But you just see me as a slave,
A worthless but amusing knave.

You say I always let you down,
That I am just a useless clown,
Why must you treat me with such scorn,
When to you, my soul I've sworn.

Perhaps I'll just admit defeat,
Your stony heart I cannot beat,
But when I'm gone, please recall,
The one who offered you his all.

Nigel Purssell

FRIENDSHIP

Friendship is precious yet cannot be bought.
Friendship is there but has to be sought.
Make an acquaintance - just say 'hello' -
In no time at all this is someone you know.

A friendship is forming that could last for years
Bringing you happiness, sharing your tears.
Friendship is special, friendship is rare,
Yet it costs nothing to show that you care.

Friendship won't recognise colour or race,
Only the smile it can put on your face.
What does it matter as long as you're kind?
Hold out your hand for friendship to find.

A friend who is rich may one day be poor
But friendship will welcome him still to your door.
For friendship to flourish and never to end,
Remember the rule - you must first <u>be</u> a friend.

Carol Ratcliffe

'DIVINE CREATOR'

When I'm looking for the answers
When things seem so unfair
I call upon The Lord above
I know He's always there.

When I need His reassurance
When I'm questioning and broken
My Lord, He always speaks to me
Yet His answers are unspoken.

He's my favourite of all teachers
And a very special friend
He was there at the beginning
And He'll be there at the end.

Nicki Rhodes-Foster

'THE ARRIVAL'

Heard the 'stork' has just arrived
And with it brought you joy
A tiny bundle with bright eyes
One happy baby boy.

He's been a long time coming
But now that he is here
Mum can have a cup of tea
And Dad a pint of beer.

A new life is so precious
You can't believe your eyes
Of all life's wondrous happenings
You've just won the first prize.

A good name has been chosen
To guide this child through life
But yet in just one short score year
He may bring home a wife!

For soon he'll be a toddler
A school boy then to work
And as those years fly by him
He may drive you berserk.

So as you gaze into his cot
And wonder what you've done
Just sit back, and take your time
Enjoy this boy, your son.

Anne E. Roberts

BACK TO BASICS

Often today, sadly we see
The break-up of the family
Bringing so much misery.
Lacking compromise maybe?
For many folk unfortunately
Life isn't all it could be.
In this materialistic society
Ever-wanting, often needlessly.
On television foolishly
Audiences scream hysterically,
For costly prizes given free
Paid by consumers eventually,
Both Education and Health Service plea
For greater help financially,
Pay extra tax, why cannot we?
There's money for the Lottery,
Where is our priority?
Politician's appeal hopefully
Back to basics, we should agree,
By example do we see
Signs of their sincerity?
Extremes of wealth and poverty
Divide us continually
Fairness: Justice: there must be
To achieve, a closer unity.

Ted Rogers

TALES OF AN AIRMAN

An airman is he King of the sky,
Flying his Robin every so high.
Free as a bird he wings his way,
Up in the clouds maketh his day.
Speeding along never a care,
Suddenly turbulence disturbs the air.
Says to himself 'how very unkind,
That's put my schedule some what behind.'
Then an Air-Cruiser comes into view,
Calm and collected he knows what to do
Contact control roger and out,
He's been informed to turn roundabout.
Sorry said they you can't land at Southend,
It should be O.K. if you fly to Ostend.
Telephones his dear wife says I'll be home late,
Who exclaims to their son well isn't that great!
The dinner is cooked will be too spoiled to eat,
The cat purr's in hope of another late treat,
Its part of the price an Airman must pay,
Endless surprises happen that way.

Ted Rogers

TEARS OF A CLOWN

The tears of a clown when all alone
Come tumbling down
With the hurt and the pain

The smile of a clown so obvious and bold
When really
There is another story to be told

The eyes of a clown so wide and bright
When all of the time
They see no light

The heart of a clown hidden from sight
Is breaking and aching
Both day and night

The tears of a clown
Could be bottled and sold
For they are more precious than gold.

Sharon Rosenwould

STAND BACK

Thoughts go around
Words unspoken
When you do let go
Its just a token

I hear the thoughts
Spoken words a blur
Its between the lines
On me there's a slur

Is that really me
The picture I paint
Look at the lines
Are they really so faint

Stand back
Take a closer look
Am I so different
From when the vows I took

Forsaking all others
I said it out loud
Next to our witnesses
In front of the crowd

Is the picture I paint
Really so black
Or have I gone abstract
All front to back

Stand back take another look
I'll do the same
Its life together
Not a game.

Sharon Rosenwould

MY MEMORY

Something happened to me:
It stopped me sleeping for a time,
Long but not long ago -
Then I reclaimed my mind.

I'm having dreams about it now,
My dictionary said:
Previous memories will return
And mutilate your head.

I know my memory will go away
Once I have spoken of my misery,
But every time I try to let it flow
My throat goes dry, my eyes well - up
My thoughts start to twist and churn and the other person becomes less
Concerned - if I laugh,
And inside I'm spinning, like a child's spinning - top.

Sometimes, like last night,
I feel like letting go
Cast myself off,
Drift away -
Escape
Survival.
Go.

So left here, nervously waiting,
Saying my dazed goodbyes
Into darkness, I disappear
All that's left are my wide, staring eyes.

Sabby

ANOTHER RIOT!!!

Another riot!!! It cannot be,
Not in this land we love so dear.
Another riot!!! Why can't they see,
That we now live in a world of fear.

Once this peaceful country
Showed the world just how to live,
Side by side united
With only love to give.

Gone are the days when we used to take a stroll across the park,
Now no one dares to walk unaccompanied in the dark.

Another riot!!! What will they gain,
This self destruction, causes sorrow and such pain.
Slowly England's dying,
As we watch helpless and afraid.
Afraid of what might happen in the next viscous, bloody, raid.

This rioting's like a cancer creeping slowly in our midst,
And like the dreaded illness as, yet no cure exists.
But somehow we must find a way
Without prejudice or lies,
Or very soon this land we love
Will die before our eyes.

Maureen Salmon

DISCOVERY

Deep within a fragile heart
A special love has grown.
Love so sweet and natural
To me you've gently shown.
What is this strange feeling
That sends my mind a reeling.
A gentle touch, a whispered word,
Long since heard.
A secret smile, a loving kiss,
Long since missed.
This joy I feel
Fits me like a glove
What is it
Simply love.

Brenda Saxty

WHODINNI'S DREAM?

As concrete shadows cease to follow,
Day's empty desires, they turn to wallow.
And drift from toxic residence to feast,
On memories of once protesting beasts.

Resting on clouds, caressing their harps,
They encounter, with green anticipation.
The crystal serenity of filtered hearts,
Through chained emancipation.
Where endless landscapes meet cherished skies,
And velvet skin is lost in passionate eyes.

Momentary beauty is all for some,
Whose mortal dream has yet to come,

Marco Scarola

THE SILENT LAND (ABOUT DEATH)

Do you see me I wonder?
I come here every night, if only
I can comfort you, and try to ease your plight.

I watched you in the churchyard,
And saw the tears you shed,
But do not grieve, or feel so sad.
Better to remember me and smile,
Than to be sad.
I am in the silent land,
A place that is unseen.
I took my leave, and travelled here,
And now am free from pain.
A soul has many paths to travel,
To where, we cannot tell,
Perhaps we will meet one day soon
In future times to come.
The silent land is all around us
With birds and beast, and flowers,
We watch, we see, but do not judge,
So do not be sad,
Remember, I still can see your lovely face,
So wipe away those tears reunited we will be
In the silent land one day,
Better to remember me and 'Smile,
Than be sad.'

Jennifer Sharp

HOME -SWEET- HOME

Home is a place where we like to stay,
A place for children to grow and play.
Home is a place for us to sleep,
Where families learn to love and weep;

It matters not if you are rich or poor,
As long as it has an open door,
So folk can visit any old time
Joys and sorrows can be shared with mine.

Children too, bring their problems home,
From time to time they like to roam,
If they are sad and feeling low
Its Home - Sweet - Home they choose to go;

Some emigrate to pastures new,
You miss the things you used to do,
Holidays in summer, with family, by the sea;
Now Home - Sweet - Home will always hold
Those memories for me.

Gladys Sharp

MONOLOGUE FOR A NEW LOVER

There is a life within me
That only you breathe into me
It is an uncontrollable love for you
Which with every touch, kiss and memory,
Is enhanced and defined
Sculptures spend hours
Trying to stop, the way I feel now.
Writers use such complex terms,
To confuse such a simple issue
This is not meant to cast fear -
My eyes are quit and placid,
Or so I've been told - Once or twice.
My only explanation is my happiness -
The way I can smile for no reason,
When you are close,
The way one mile.
May as well be a life times worth of walking,
When you are such a distance away.
I tend not to speak these thoughts
As openly as I wish to,
I open my mouth, yet the words do not frequently exit.
I enjoy, usually, to remain silent.
Yet suddenly, I find it hard to keep my peace.....
My love for you is growing....

Alison Shaw

ENCHANTMENT

She looked enchanting
As she lay there,
I could not help
Myself but stare,
Sweet sleeping beauty
You are so fine,
I shall always love you
Till the end of time.

Kim Singh

FLOWERS

Pretty flowers, dazzling colours, red, blue, yellow, white.
Tease the eye and please the mind and as day takes over night.
Scented smells waft from within to draw the bees to feed
Silently persuading them to carry away their seed.
Some grow wild and some are grown to bring happiness and love.
Is there a message in the flower, sent from up above?
They can put a cheer in a dismal room. A smile on a person who is ill.
Say a message of sorry or get well soon. Happy birthday just to thrill.
Flowers can do many things in ways we just don't know.
Like showing hearts that they are loved. Good bye to those that must
Go.
The flower however small it may be can only be unique.
It cheers us up. It tells us things and it doesn't need to speak.
A flower only grows I'm sure to bring happiness abound.
A little tender life form from deep within the ground.
When life for you takes a downward turn and things begin to sour.
Stretch out your hand as you bend down and pick a lovely flower.

William Singleton

CLOUDS

Fluffy white continents drift across sky.
Changing images in the mind's eye.
Faces of people that we thought we knew.
Great cuddly toys in a backdrop of blue.
Some carry water how precious the rain.
Some shade the sun's rays that can bring us much pain.
They drift across oceans and over land.
Clouds have no boundaries they don't understand.
Just rolling through life in an endless demand.
Carried by winds that can be severe.
Forcing them there and blowing them here.
Clouds are so huge that they always seem low.
But where do they hide and where do they go.
They are light and so fluffy, and too big to miss.
They are here then they are gone just as quick as a kiss.

William Singleton

WINTER COMING

Leaves dropping, wind blowing;
Winter fast draws near.
Light failing, rain driving,
Herald the end of the year.

Frost spreading, mist hanging;
Winter gets a grip.
Water freezing, ponds glazing,
Children run, slide and skip.

Snow falling, fog hugging;
Winter takes its toll.
Cold chilling, ice creeping,
Outside ventures not a soul.

Storm howling, blizzard blasting;
Winter's grip grows tight
Gale gusting, tempest tossing
As day turns to harsher night.

Night covering, darkness hiding;
Winter is ally to night.
Frost freezing, ice icing,
I'm glad I'm at home this night

Christopher Stavrou

WILL YOU

Will you walk with me across the land,
And when it's dark hold my hand.

Will you keep me safe and warm, and shelter me
Throughout the storm.

Will you take away my fear and say the thing's I
Need to hear.

Will you get bored with the thing's I say,
Can you get me through the day.

Nicola Stewart

ALIVE AGAIN

Like a stranger in a crowd I see you for the first time
Love or fascination? Boy I wish you were mine
I look forward to catching a glimpse of you I don't know your name
The thrill and romance is in the chase its like a game
I see you walking towards me my hearts beating faster and faster
Like a tongue tied fool I speak to you what a disaster
I was blinded by your beauty you drive me out of my mind
A charming woman you are and unselfishly kind
Found out your name your the one I like the best
I respect the colour of your skin you retain my interest
You really are gorgeous you have a wonderful personality
You're always in my thoughts that's the effect you have on me.

Love or lust? How I would love to hold you and kiss you passionately
Caress and make love to your naked coloured body tenderly
Happily married family woman you are unfortunately that's true
Much to my disappointment I can never have you
Different backgrounds cultures colour and race
Nevertheless I still look forward to seeing that smiling face
Witty funny intelligent caring that's your way
When I see you I come alive again you brighten up my day
Surely you must feel the attraction or is it just wishful thinking on my
Part
Happy valentines you've touched a special place deep within my heart.

Brian Stoneman

SURFING

Surely, the tide, as surely as my life
At this place where dreams must end
And all fears come. Oh, how I wished
Things different, waters of the womb
Taken me to another place than such waves
Dragging me down! And I see your face
In a brave moon straining to catch
The dawn. As would I, or I die,
Surely, the tide, as surely as dreams
Of fame, fortune, someone to care;
When they laughed, you shrugged the score
Taking on more than I bargained for
And I wouldn't chance your blushes
But hung back, to let you ride white horses
With the pack - to hell and back!
Surely, our lives, as surely as pride
Picking at my bones. I love you!
Yet only had time for this tide's amen
None for its daily giving and taking;
You shy like a wild thing at the world's taunts
Refuse to be dragged into line, braving
Heaven head - on. Now! A sure tide's surfing me.
Where I want to be, with you!
Who wore a sandman's mask but tore it off
To prove how some dreams last;
Soulmates, drowning in the world's nightmares
Saved! On this, our first BIG wave.

Roger N. Taber

MIDGE

Our jumbo Yorkie - Midge by name, had really gone to seed,
With matted hair and perfume rare attention she did need.
Her bedraggled state would quite deter the eager hand to pat
Not like a dog at all she looked, more like an old door-mat.
I pondered on her sorry state, and thought it must be soon,
To get an expert on the job at a canine beauty salon.

A lady from that establishment arrived just one hour late,
And took Midge off in the back of her car, a new image to create.
Collect and deliver is the service which they bestow on one,
I waited home expectantly to see what they had done.
At last a car drew to a halt outside our front door gate,
Out jumped Midge, I knew her not-first class at Crufts she'd rate.

All her hair was clipped away, her eyes at last were seen,
In truth I wished that she still looked the way she'd always been.
Her talons long, they all were gone, of this I was quite glad,
For the noise upon the kitchen floor would nearly drive you mad.
How sad she now looks sitting there, her breed it looks quite rare,
I'd swear it was someone else's dog, no more our woolly bear.

Now dogs don't like being laughed at, as everybody knows,
So no more walks in daylight hours until her new hair grows.
Abandoned I am sure she'll feel when I go out to shop,
But if she knew what she looked like, at home she'd gladly stop.
This expert who her image changed said in three months time she'd Call,
To take Midge off to her beauty salon for a further overhaul,
I decided loud and clear, maybe I was abrupt,
At home I would keep my Yorkie when she had her next scrub-up.

Mary Tevlin

THINGS WE'LL SHARE

A gentle word when the day is through
Now and then a smile or two
A warm embrace when work is through
These are the things we'll share
The giving in to whims and woes
The joy of buying baby clothes
A love like ours that grows and grows
These are the things we'll share
An understanding point of view
A kiss each night and morning to
To hold you close when the day is through
These are the things we'll share
And when it comes that we must part
Where ever you go you'll take my heart
That's when our life here is through
Just remember I love you
These are the things we'll share.

William Tremlett

THAT CERTAIN AGE

When in life you've reached that certain age
Life reads like that of a history page
Each page having a story to be told
With happy and sad secrets it does hold
As a child most memories are sweet
Happy days and a special treat
With the gift of learning bestowed by Him above
And the joy or frustration of that first love
Then in life comes that special day
When you promise to love honour and obey
With the building of a home, both to share
And the coming of children, whom to love and care
To guide them through life to be honest and true
And the gift of a grandchild they give to you
Life reads like that of a history page
When in life you've reached that certain age.

William Tremlett

THE WIND

Where did it come from, where does it go
It whips up the waves, turning tides to and throw
White horses chasing across waves crest
Crashing them on rocks and sands to rest
It crosses the beach lifting the sand
Over the marsh then on to solid land
Running through the heathers and moorlands grass
Bending trees, stealing leaves as it goes past
It moves the clouds with little strain
Turning sunshine to snow, thunder or rain
Twisting and turning around the churchyard
Splashing rain on gravestone, granite hard
Running free with hate and love
With no control from Him above.

William Tremlett

SEED OF INSPIRATION

When the leaf fell from up above
And landed on my golden locks
The seed of inspiration was sown
And poetry from my soul began to flow
Full of verse and rhyming words
Upon your ears they were meant to be heard
Many words of love and hate
Was it destined to be my fate
Sometimes feeling high and low
What emotions lie deep down below
Sadness and happiness emerging from time to time
To be merry and cheerful that aim is mine.

Marilyn Ward

LONELINESS

From day to day I sit here all alone
And no-one calls me on the phone
The silence of this house I bear
All day long I sit and stare
I wonder what the future brings
Upon my fingers I wear no rings
All my life I've tried to find
A love that I feel won't die
Possibly easier said than done
No man's heart have I won
They've never held my hand and said
I love you my dear let's get wed
So here I sit alone am I
The years go by and time just flies
Sad and lonely old and grey
I've been alone everyday.

Marilyn Ward

MESSAGE

If you really care about me,
You will pass this on.
Send it to the one I love,
Right after I am gone.

I write upon this paper,
The emotions that I feel.
Before my deaths upon me,
For my heart can never heal.

Take care of them forever,
Make sure they do not pine.
Keep them away from anguish,
And hope they remain all mine.

Julia Wells

A HERMIT

I am a hermit, I live alone,
Cramped up in four walls, that
I now call my home.
If someone passes they might stop and chat,
Or kick at me, when I'm lying flat.

Some people are not as lucky, I know,
They have no place at all to go.
People do not give generously, to individuals like me.
Not even one big cardboard box.

Some people spit, some yell out
'Why don't you go to work instead
Of cluttering up the pavement with your bed?'

If I had a house or even a flat,
Given any old job, even minding a cat,
I wouldn't be a hermit living alone
Cramped up in four walls that I now call my home.

Holli Wells

A TEAR

Tell me what you see,
When you look at me?
Do you see a person
Full of bravery?

Do you see a person,
Who you want to know?
Or do you just see me
And what I tell you so?

Is it just an image,
I put before you here?
As you turn and walk away,
I wipe away a tear.

You used to make me feel,
Like I could be a saint,
But now that you are gone,
My images are faint.

For what I used to know,
Now is just a dream.
I can only hope and pray
That truth will rule supreme.

When you and I were two,
It took away my fear.
But now that I am one,
I wipe away a tear.

Julia Wells

THE WIND

Whirling, whistling, searching through the trees the raw wind
Drives.
Sweeping unsuspecting leaves, like bees up from their hive.
Rattling at the windows, tormenting every branch.
Gushing, threatening, bending flowers, forcing them to dance.
Racing down the chimney stacks, bashing unlocked gates.
Crashing, screaming, howling like ghosts midst strong debate.
Wrecking, fast destroying all that occupies its course,
Like angry dog it fiercely growls boasting of its force.
Cracking fences, uprooting trees, marring all it finds.
Then disappears without a trace, destruction left behind.

Marie Williams

INDECENT BEHAVIOUR?

Approach the bench and take the stand.
As I declare my love for you
Is like a baron distant land.
I tell you your honour, that statement's true!
Take into account that I once knew
That person accused of stealing my light,
For I did not know that saying 'I do'
Would lead to that woman blinding my sight.
I address the jury to study my plight,
For she used a mild form of corruption.
So try as I might to put up a fight,
I was powerless against her seduction.
Deliver your verdict with caution and favour,
For love will not punish indecent behaviour.

Anthony Williams